Original title:
When We Were Us

Copyright © 2024 Swan Charm
All rights reserved.

Author: Mirell Mesipuu
ISBN HARDBACK: 978-9916-79-209-4
ISBN PAPERBACK: 978-9916-79-210-0
ISBN EBOOK: 978-9916-79-211-7

Chronicle of Our Celestial Dance

In the heavens, we twirl with grace,
Stars whisper secrets in sacred space.
Each step we take, a prayer aligned,
Echoes of love in shadows entwined.

As moonlight bathes our souls anew,
We find our path in the morning dew.
With every heartbeat, we rise and sway,
In divine rhythm, come what may.

The Anointed Ties of Yesterday

Threads of faith weave through our past,
In tapestries where shadows cast.
We gather the lessons, our hearts expand,
With every memory, we take a stand.

Anointed souls in twilight glow,
Embracing the truths from long ago.
Bound together by love's sweet thread,
We rise with the sun, where hope is spread.

Eternal Echoes of Shared Beliefs

In the stillness, our spirits sing,
Binding us close, like treasure's ring.
Echoes resound from ages past,
In shared beliefs, our roots hold fast.

With whispered prayers, we touch the skies,
In unity, our purpose lies.
Hand in hand, through trials we tread,
In love, our eternal truths are bred.

Sacred Garlands of Memory

Beneath the boughs of the ancient tree,
We weave our stories, wild and free.
Garlands of memory, fragrant and bright,
A tapestry glows in the soft twilight.

With each bloom that opens, a tale unfolds,
Of hope, of sorrow, in whispers told.
The sacred bonds of our cherished ties,
In the garden of heart, our spirit flies.

The Everlasting Embrace of Hope

In shadows deep, a light appears,
To guide the lost through vale of tears.
With open arms, the heavens call,
Embracing dreams that rise and fall.

Through trials faced and battles fought,
A whisper speaks, our fears are sought.
Resilience blooms, a garden rare,
In faith we stand, our souls laid bare.

Beneath the storm, we'll seek our peace,
In every heartbeat, love's increase.
For in the dark, a seed is sown,
Hope's tender grace, we call our own.

The Liturgy of Our Bond

Together we gather, hand in hand,
In sacred moments, we take our stand.
With every word, our spirits rise,
In prayerful song, we touch the skies.

Each breath a hymn, a shared decree,
In unity's fold, we dare to be.
With hearts aligned, we seek the light,
In love's embrace, we draw from night.

Through trials shared, our faith grows bold,
In whispered truths, our stories told.
Together we weave a tapestry bright,
The threads of hope, entwined in light.

A Pilgrim's Prayer of Remembrance

O gentle Spirit, guide my way,
Through paths unknown, where shadows play.
For every step, I seek your grace,
In echoes past, I find my place.

Each memory a lantern's glow,
Illuminating all I know.
With humble heart, I sing your praise,
Through nights of doubt, through sunlit days.

As arching skies give testament,
To every soul, through time well spent.
In reverence deep, I lift my voice,
For in the past, we find our choice.

Sanctifying the Echoes of Yesterday

In every whisper, time revered,
A sacred bond, forever cleared.
For memories hold a gentle sway,
In hallowed ground, we find our way.

From trials faced to joys we've known,
In every seed of love we've sown.
The echoes call, as spirits rise,
In faith's embrace, we touch the skies.

Through stones of time, in unity,
We sculpt our dreams, in harmony.
Each moment blessed, a gift divine,
In echoes past, our hearts entwine.

The Sacred Dance of Our Intertwined Paths

In whispers soft, the Spirit moves,
Guiding souls through sacred grooves.
Each step a prayer, each turn divine,
In the dance of life, our hearts entwine.

With faith as our rhythm, we sway in grace,
Embracing the Light in this sacred space.
Hands joined in unity, our voices sing,
Echoing love in the joy we bring.

Through trials faced, we find our way,
In the arms of hope, forever we stay.
Bound by trust like the stars above,
In this sacred dance, we find our love.

Let mercy flow in every embrace,
Creating a bond that time can't erase.
Together we journey, together we roam,
In the sacred dance, we find our home.

Heavenly Reverberations of Our Joy

In the morning light, our spirits soar,
With laughter ringing on heaven's floor.
Angels rejoice in the sound we make,
Celebrating love in every heartbeat's ache.

With grateful hearts, we raise our song,
A harmony sweet, where we all belong.
Each note a blessing, each word a prayer,
In the symphony of life, we are laid bare.

Through trials faced, our faith remains,
A testament strong against life's pains.
Together we stand, united and bold,
In the heavenly chorus that never grows old.

As seasons change, our hope ignites,
Guiding us through the darkest nights.
In joy we gather, in grace we find,
Heavenly reverberations, ever entwined.

The Sanctuary of Shared Breath

In the hush of twilight, our hearts align,
A sanctuary built, so divine.
Through quiet whispers, we find our rest,
In the sacred space, love is confessed.

Each breath we share a gift from above,
Nurtured in patience, wrapped in love.
Facing the world with courage anew,
In this sanctuary, we are true.

Bound by the essence of soft-spoken grace,
We find our rhythm, we find our place.
With open arms, we gather near,
In the sanctuary of breath, we are clear.

With every heartbeat, the bond will grow,
In this sacred haven, we come to know.
Through trials and triumphs, together we tread,
In the sanctuary of shared breath, we are led.

The Pilgrimage of Our Love

On paths untrodden, we set our feet,
In the pilgrimage of love, our souls meet.
With lanterns of faith, we light the way,
Guided by hope, come what may.

Through valleys of shadows, hand in hand,
We traverse the terrain, a sacred land.
Each step a promise, each mile a vow,
In the pilgrimage of love, we learn how.

With hearts as compasses, we journey forth,
Cherishing moments of immeasurable worth.
In the echoes of silence, our spirits unite,
In this pilgrimage of love, we find our light.

As seasons change, our vision stays clear,
With love as our guide, we conquer fear.
Through mountains and rivers, we'll ever remain,
In the pilgrimage of love, enduring the strain.

Pilgrimage of Togetherness through Time

In the dawn's early light we tread,
Together we walk, with hearts widespread.
Each step a prayer, each breath a song,
In unity's embrace, where we belong.

Through valleys deep and mountains high,
We gather our hopes under a vast sky.
The years may pass, yet here we stand,
Hand in hand, in this sacred land.

Through trials faced and battles fought,
In love's pure vessel, our souls are caught.
A tapestry woven with threads of grace,
Endless journeys, a shared embrace.

The whispers of ages guide our way,
With faith as our anchor, come what may.
Together we move, as one we shine,
In the pilgrimage of hearts divine.

With each dawn rising, a chance to share,
In moments tender, in sincere prayer.
The road ahead may twist and wind,
But together, the light we will find.

The Grace of Our Laughter Resounds

In the heart of joy, our voices unite,
Laughter like echoes, a pure delight.
With every chuckle, the spirit takes flight,
A symphony of grace in radiant light.

Gathered in circles, our stories unfold,
In warmth and wonder, our bonds are told.
The joy of the moment, a divine embrace,
In the laughter of friends, we find our place.

Through trials of life, in shadows and sun,
Together we stand, though battles be won.
With each shared smile, a blessing bestowed,
In the grace of our laughter, love is flowed.

In whispers of joy, in tears set free,
In the grace of our laughter, we find the key.
Together we celebrate, the gift of today,
In moments so precious, we come what may.

Each joyful note a prayer of its own,
In the symphony of love, we are never alone.
Bound by the laughter that bubbles and swells,
In the grace of our joy, true harmony dwells.

Transcendent Bonds in the Realm of Faith

In the quiet night, our spirits entwine,
Transcendent bonds, through space and time.
Unseen threads connect, and hearts align,
In the realm of faith, our hopes brightly shine.

With whispers soft, we share our dreams,
Faith's gentle current flows in streams.
Across the chasms, through shadows cast,
Our bonds transcend, united at last.

In trials faced, through fire and storm,
Together we rise, in love's true form.
The light of belief, a beacon ablaze,
In the depths of our souls, it ever stays.

Hand in hand, we traverse the night,
In the warmth of our faith, we seek the light.
With every prayer, our spirits soar,
In the realm of love, we open the door.

With grace we journey, through strife and peace,
In transcendent bonds, we find release.
The sacred connection, in the heart's domain,
Together in faith, we break every chain.

A Communion of Hearts Beneath the Moon

Beneath the moon's glow, we gather as one,
In a communion of hearts, our fears come undone.
With starlit whispers, our spirits embrace,
In the night's gentle cradle, we find our place.

Under silvery beams, our stories unfold,
Each heartfelt sharing, a treasure untold.
With laughter and tears, we weave our prayer,
In the moonlight's glow, our burdens we share.

As shadows dance lightly upon the ground,
In this sacred circle, peace is found.
With faith as our guide, we sing to the night,
In the communion of souls, we find our light.

Through the stillness, the wisdom flows free,
In the bonds of our gathering, we come to see.
The love that surrounds us, a radiant bloom,
Together we flourish, dispelling the gloom.

A prayer on each breath, a song in the heart,
In communion and love, we'll never part.
Beneath the vast heavens, so gently we swoon,
Embraced by the light of the ever-bright moon.

The Hymn of Our Harmonized Souls

In the stillness, we pray,
Hearts entwined, seek the way.
Voices rise in sacred song,
Together, where we belong.

Stars above, shining bright,
Guiding us through the night.
With each word, love unfolds,
A tapestry of souls.

Grace flows like a gentle stream,
Binding us in a divine dream.
Harmony echoes through time,
In unity, we find our rhyme.

In the valley, we find peace,
From our worries, we release.
Hands held high, we make a vow,
To cherish the sacred now.

Through the trials, we shall stand,
Faith and hope, hand in hand.
In this hymn, our hearts align,
Forever, in love divine.

Prayerful Reflections in the Waters of Time

In quiet moments, we reflect,
On the love that we connect.
Ripples stirred by each soft prayer,
Carried high on gentle air.

The past whispers, tales unfold,
In the waters, truths are told.
Mirrored depths where shadows play,
Guided by the light of day.

Every tear, a lesson learned,
In our hearts, the fire burned.
Waves of joy and sorrow blend,
In this journey, we transcend.

As time dances, we embrace,
Every challenge, a sacred grace.
Holding fast to faith's embrace,
In the waters, find our place.

With each heartbeat, love's refrain,
Guides us through the joy and pain.
Together, we shall forever climb,
In the waters, prayers in time.

Communion of Hearts Under Divine Light

Beneath the stars, hearts ignite,
In communion, we share light.
Souls attuned to the divine,
In this space, our spirits shine.

From shadows cast, we emerge,
Unified by love's sweet surge.
In every glance, a sacred spark,
Guided forth, no longer dark.

Voices blend in soft refrain,
Whispers carried like the rain.
Sharing burdens, lifting souls,
Together, we make each other whole.

In the silence, we find grace,
Every heartbeat, a warm embrace.
Underneath the endless skies,
Love's reflection never lies.

With hearts open, we shall soar,
Finding peace forevermore.
In this communion, hearts unite,
Forever bask in the purest light.

Sacred Chronicles of Love's Evolution

In the gardens where we bloom,
Stories weave, dispelling gloom.
Each moment, a precious page,
In the book of love, we gauge.

Through trials faced, we have grown,
In our hearts, seeds of love sown.
Every chapter rich and true,
Bound by faith, we start anew.

As time unfolds, we discover,
The strength found in one another.
In love's light, we take our stand,
Hand in hand, we understand.

From whispers shared in the night,
To dawn's embrace, eternal light.
Sacred chronicles we write,
In each heart, a guiding sight.

Together, we celebrate,
The evolution of our fates.
In harmony, we'll forever sing,
Our love, a sacred offering.

The Divine Tapestry of Our Existence

In the loom of grace, we are spun,
Every thread in rhythm, woven as one.
The colors of faith, bright and bold,
Unraveling tales of love to behold.

In the shadows and light, we seek the way,
Guided by whispers of the heavens' sway.
Each moment a stitch in the garment of time,
Awakening souls to reason and rhyme.

Beneath the stars, our spirits align,
Intertwined destinies by the grand design.
From the fibers of hope, we rise and mend,
Embracing life's journey, hand in hand we send.

In the dance of existence, we learn to trust,
In the embrace of mercy, we are born from dust.
The divine fabric holds us, firm and tight,
Together we journey, into the light.

Our hearts are the needles, piercing through pain,
Sewing love's lessons, joy and gain.
In the tapestry vast, we find our place,
A masterpiece woven by a loving grace.

Reflections in the Celestial Waters of Love.

In the stillness of night, love's waters gleam,
Mirroring souls, like a heavenly dream.
We gather at shores where hearts softly sigh,
In each gentle wave, our spirits comply.

Beneath the moon's glow, we whisper our vows,
The stars bear witness to what love allows.
Ripples of kindness flow wide and far,
In the depths of compassion, we reveal who we are.

As the tides of time ebb and flow,
Each reflection reveals how we grow.
In the currents of grace, we find our way,
Floating on faith, come what may.

In the embrace of silence, love speaks clear,
Echoes of laughter that only hearts hear.
In celestial waters, we lose and we find,
The treasures of love, intertwined and kind.

Together we voyage, hearts joined as one,
In the dance of the cosmos, our journey's begun.
Every drop, a prayer sent up from below,
In love's pure reflection, we flourish and glow.

Elysian Echoes of Togetherness

In the gardens of grace, we find our song,
Where every soul's heartbeat feels like a throng.
Echoes of joy cascade through the air,
In togetherness, we banish despair.

Hand in hand, we weave our dreams,
Through valleys of hope, where sunlight beams.
With each gentle whisper, a promise made,
In the symphony of love, none are afraid.

The laughter is our anthem, resounding bright,
A chorus of spirits, united in light.
Through trials and triumphs, we hold each other,
In the embrace of kin, sister and brother.

As the seasons change and time marches on,
Our bond only deepens, the love still strong.
With every heartbeat, a story unveiled,
In the book of togetherness, we shall not fail.

With eyes lifted high to the heavens above,
We honor the journey, the gifts of our love.
In the dance of existence, we're never apart,
Elysian echoes resound in the heart.

Sacred Threads of Our Embrace

In the circle of life, our souls intertwine,
With sacred threads of love, perfectly aligned.
Each heartbeat a promise, a story untold,
In the warmth of our embrace, we find the gold.

With arms open wide, we gather near,
In moments of joy, and in times of fear.
A tapestry of memories crafted with care,
Every stitch a testament of love we share.

Through storms that may come, we stand as one,
In the name of compassion, our battle is won.
The fabric is strong, together we rise,
With hope in our hearts and faith in our eyes.

In the quiet of night, when shadows descend,
Our love forms a shield, a means to defend.
In the weaving of time, our journey flows,
Sacred threads of our embrace, a love that glows.

Though life may be fleeting, our spirits will soar,
For in the embrace of love, we are forevermore.
In each gentle weave, the promise of grace,
Anchored in faith, we find our place.

Holy Reverie of Days Long Past

In whispers soft, the angels sing,
We gather 'round, their praises bring.
Each moment cherished, lost in grace,
A journey traced in sacred space.

Through valleys deep, and mountains high,
The echoes of our faith comply.
In shadows cast, the light shall glow,
Remembering paths we used to know.

With every prayer, a bond we weave,
In holy reverie, we believe.
A tapestry of grace untold,
In memories, we find our gold.

Let silence speak in gentle tones,
Where love resounds among the stones.
The past remains, our guiding star,
In every heart, near or far.

With gratitude, our voices rise,
An anthem sweet, beyond the skies.
For days long past, we offer praise,
In holy reverie, we gaze.

The Blessing of Shared Dreams

In the stillness, our hearts align,
Whispers of hope through the divine.
Together we walk, a sacred thread,
In shared dreams, our spirits are fed.

Through trials faced, we stand as one,
In unity, the work is done.
With open arms, and faith so strong,
We find the place where we belong.

Blessings flow like rivers wide,
In every step, the Light's our guide.
With laughter shared, and tears we shed,
In each moment, the Spirit's fed.

Each story told brings us closer,
A fragrant rose, a kind exposure.
In dreams we build, love's gentle scheme,
Forever bound in shared dream team.

We navigate this sacred dance,
Held in grace, we take our chance.
For in our hearts, there lies the flame,
The blessing found in love's sweet name.

Spiritual Footprints on Sacred Ground

With every step, our path unfolds,
In sacred ground, a truth reveals.
The footprints marked, a sign of grace,
In nature's arms, we find our place.

The rustle of leaves, a soft embrace,
Each breath we take, a gift we trace.
In quiet whispers, wisdom speaks,
The love we seek, the heart it seeks.

In sunlight's glow, our spirits soar,
With open hearts, we find the door.
To realms of peace, forever blessed,
In every moment, we find rest.

As seasons change, so do our souls,
In unity, the Spirit rolls.
Through valleys low and peaks so grand,
We walk together, hand in hand.

With gratitude, we mark the ground,
In each heartbeat, the love is found.
These footprints left, a legacy,
In sacred ground, we'll always be.

A Tapestry of Time and Tenderness

In threads of gold, our stories weave,
A tapestry, we all believe.
With every sorrow, joy unfolds,
In love's embrace, the heart consoled.

Through gentle hands, and caring hearts,
Each moment shared, a work of art.
In laughter bright, and tears that flow,
The fabric of our lives shall grow.

With whispers soft, we write our tale,
In kindness' name, we shall prevail.
Each stitch a prayer, a hope so bright,
In darkness, we become the light.

In every season, change we find,
Together woven, souls entwined.
In love's sweet rhythm, we shall dance,
A tapestry of life's romance.

As we embrace the gift of time,
In every heartbeat, love's sweet rhyme.
A story old, yet ever new,
In tenderness, our journey's true.

Reverent Reflections of Unity

In the quiet of the night, we pray,
Voices rising, kept at bay.
Hearts entwined in sacred song,
Together we stand, forever strong.

By the light of the faithful flame,
We gather close, calling His name.
In harmony, our spirits soar,
A bond unbroken, forevermore.

Through trials and sorrows, we find peace,
In love's embrace our fears release.
With open hands, we share our grace,
In every heart, He finds a place.

As we walk upon this earthly shore,
With eyes uplifted, we seek the core.
In unity's rhythm, we find our way,
Reflecting His light, come what may.

The Holy Altar of Our Affections

At the altar where we lay our dreams,
Embers flicker, hope gently gleams.
Every whisper of devotion's breath,
In sacred silence, we conquer death.

With hearts wide open, we place our fears,
Finding solace in gentle tears.
In unity, our spirits rise,
As faith descends from the azure skies.

Each prayer a thread that weaves our lives,
In the fabric of love, our spirit thrives.
Through trials faced, through joys proclaimed,
In God's embrace, we are unashamed.

On this holy ground, we stand in light,
Warmed by the flame of love's true sight.
In every heartbeat, in every glance,
We find our peace in sacred dance.

Celestial Harmonies of Our Hearts

In the stillness, angels sing,
A melody of hope, a sacred thing.
With every note, our souls entwine,
In celestial harmonies, divine.

When shadows fall and doubts arise,
We listen close to faith's sweet cries.
In the silence, love's light grows,
Guiding us where the spirit flows.

As stars align in the midnight sky,
Each twinkle whispers, "Do not shy."
In the gathering glow of grace,
We find our strength in this holy space.

Through every trial, through every test,
In the arms of love, we find our rest.
Celestial chords of joy we sing,
In unity, our spirits take wing.

Remnants of a Sacred Journey

As we wander through valleys deep,
In faith, we sow the seeds we keep.
Each footfall a testament to grace,
On this sacred journey, we find our place.

With every sunrise, hearts ignite,
Guided by hope's everlasting light.
In the tapestry of life, we weave,
Through every loss, we still believe.

The whispers of the past remain,
In memories sweet, joy mingles with pain.
Each smile a tribute, each tear a prayer,
In this sacred dance, love is laid bare.

Through mountains high and rivers wide,
Together we walk, side by side.
For in the remnants of days gone by,
We chart a path where spirits fly.

Sacred Stories Burnt in Time

In whispers soft, the past does speak,
Of ancient truths, both strong and weak.
Through trials faced, our spirits rise,
Holding close to faith, beneath wide skies.

Each page a flame, the heart ignites,
Illuminating darkened nights.
In every lesson, a thread to find,
The sacred stories, burnt in time.

With every prayer, the moments blend,
In sacred flames, our souls transcend.
The echoes of ages, sweet and clear,
In stories told, we hold them dear.

From ashes born, a promise gleams,
Awakening hope and fervent dreams.
As time rolls on, these tales we weave,
In faith, we gather, and we believe.

Divine Ties that Bind

In silent prayers, our hearts entwine,
Across the ages, love divine.
Through trials faced, we stand as one,
A testament to all that's done.

Embraced by grace, through storm and calm,
In every heartbeat, there lies the balm.
Together we rise, as spirits soar,
In unity's strength, we seek for more.

With every act, we weave the thread,
Of mercy showed, and kindness spread.
In every soul, a mirrored glow,
The divine ties that bind us so.

In love's embrace, our paths align,
In every moment, the stars do shine.
Through life's journey, our hands we clasp,
In faith's embrace, we'll ever last.

Holy Threads of Yesterday's Joy

In laughter bright, the spirits gleam,
In sacred moments, we share a dream.
With each sweet memory, we draw near,
The holy threads, woven so dear.

From ages past, the joy remains,
In whispered hymns, through joys and pains.
With every heartbeat, the echoes play,
In yesterday's joy, we find our way.

Through trials faced, we cherish the light,
In every dawn, the promise of night.
In love's embrace, our hearts rejoice,
In holy threads, we find our voice.

As seasons change, the joy flows on,
In every moment, where hope is drawn.
Through timeless grace, our souls align,
In yesterday's joy, forever shine.

Cherished Souls in Celestial Dance

In rhythms pure, our spirits sway,
As cherished souls, we find our way.
In sacred circles, we twirl and spin,
In heaven's light, our dance begins.

With every step, the stars ignite,
A symphony of love, a wondrous sight.
Through joy and pain, we twine as one,
In celestial dance, our hearts are spun.

In harmony's song, the universe sings,
With open arms, the joy it brings.
Through timeless grace, we lose our fears,
In cherished souls, we shed our tears.

With each embrace, the cosmos weaves,
In every rhythm, our spirit grieves.
In love's ballet, we rise above,
In cosmic dance, we find our love.

The Celestial Garden of Memories

In the stillness, whispers bloom,
Petals soft, in twilight's room.
Each memory a gentle sigh,
Reaching up to the starlit sky.

Fruits of faith, in silence found,
Roots entwined in sacred ground.
Time's embrace, a tender brush,
In the heart, sweet memories hush.

Each moment, like a fragrant rose,
Tales of love, that softly grows.
In the garden, spirits dance,
Under the gaze of divine glance.

With every tear, a seed is sown,
In this space, we are not alone.
The celestial light does guide,
In the garden where dreams abide.

Here in peace, our hearts ascend,
Embracing all, as life extends.
In every shade, a story weaves,
In the garden, our soul believes.

Divine Light in the Shadows

In the quiet dusk of night,
A glimmer shines, pure and bright.
Though shadows loom, faith ignites,
A beacon held with all our might.

With every doubt, a prayer is raised,
In the dark, our hearts are phased.
The light within, it calls us near,
Whispers of hope, calming fear.

Through valleys low, we walk with grace,
With every step, a sacred place.
Divine echoes in the air,
Holding us, a love so rare.

In trials faced, we find our road,
Carried forth by love bestowed.
The shadows shift, but cannot stay,
For light shall guide us on our way.

In the end, we shall arise,
To greet the dawn beneath the skies.
With hearts aflame, we sing our song,
In divine light, where we belong.

Anointed Ties of Affection

In the warmth of a gentle embrace,
Love's sweet touch, a sacred grace.
Bound by threads of hope and peace,
Anointed ties that never cease.

Through trials harsh and storms that rage,
Our hearts unite, we turn the page.
In laughter shared and sorrows weep,
These ties remain, steadfast and deep.

As every moment softly flows,
In unity, our spirit grows.
Like vines entwined, we find our place,
Anointed ties in love's embrace.

In whispers soft, we hear the call,
Destinies woven, through it all.
Through every tear, each joyful sigh,
These ties will never break or die.

In faith we stand, together strong,
In every heart, we find our song.
Anointed ties, forever blessed,
In love's embrace, we find our rest.

When Joys Dive into Silence

In moments still, where echoes fade,
We find the peace that joy had laid.
When laughter whispers through the air,
Silence speaks of love and care.

Each heartbeat slows, a gentle grace,
In quietude, we find our place.
When joy bows low, humility reigns,
In silent tears, the heart attains.

In twilight's glow, our thoughts entwine,
In sacred hush, we feel divine.
For in the silence, we learn to see,
The depth of joy that sets us free.

When sorrows come, and shadows loom,
In silence, we prepare our bloom.
From joys that dive, new hope arises,
In stillness found, love never disguises.

So let us dwell where silence sings,
In the heart's sanctuary, where joy springs.
For when the world grows quiet and tight,
We find our solace, in heaven's light.

The Sacred Circle of Our Lives

In the dawn's gentle light, we gather near,
Bound by a faith that casts out fear.
Each heart a lantern, each soul a guide,
In the sacred circle, where love abides.

We share our burdens, our laughter too,
Hand in hand, with skies so blue.
The whispers of nature, a tranquil song,
Together we flourish, together we're strong.

As seasons shift, our spirits rise,
In unity's embrace, the spirit flies.
In trials and triumphs, our bond we find,
In the sacred circle, forever entwined.

With every prayer, the light will grow,
With roots entwined, like rivers flow.
In moments of silence, the truth is clear,
In the sacred circle, we draw near.

So let us cherish this blessed space,
With love as the thread, our lives interlace.
In hearts' reflection, the divine does reside,
In the sacred circle, forever our guide.

Testament of Togetherness

In the quiet evening, we lift our voice,
In faith and love, we rejoice.
Each promise spoken, a bond so tight,
In the testament of togetherness, we find light.

Through valleys low and mountains high,
With prayers like stars in the night sky.
Side by side, we face the storms,
In this unity, our spirit transforms.

With hands clasped firmly, we seek the truth,
In the fires of youth, eternal proof.
In laughter shared, in tears that flow,
In the testament of togetherness, love will grow.

In every heartbeat, a message sings,
In the peace of knowing, our hope takes wings.
Through trials and joy, our spirit blends,
In the testament of togetherness, love transcends.

So let us walk, with courage and grace,
Hand in hand, we embrace.
In the light of faith, our hearts aglow,
In the testament of togetherness, we grow.

Vows Carved in Starlight

Underneath the heavens, where dreams take flight,
We etch our vows in soft starlight.
With every breath, we weave a tale,
In the tapestry of love, we shall prevail.

In whispers shared with the night breeze,
In the warmth of presence, our hearts find ease.
Each promise crafted, a guiding spark,
In vows carved in starlight, we leave a mark.

Through fleeting moments, our spirits soar,
In the quiet shadows, we yearn for more.
With faith as our anchor, we'll chart the seas,
In vows carved in starlight, our hearts find peace.

As galaxies twinkle, our hope ignites,
In love's embrace, we reach new heights.
With every heartbeat, the universe chimes,
In vows carved in starlight, we transcend time.

So let us carry this glow within,
A symphony of love, a sacred hymn.
In every moment, let gratitude bloom,
In vows carved in starlight, our spirits loom.

The Sanctity of Shared Dreams

In the garden of hope, where dreams collide,
We nurture visions, side by side.
With open hearts, we sow each seed,
In the sanctity of shared dreams, we proceed.

With every sunrise, new paths unfold,
In unity's embrace, together we're bold.
Through shadows cast, our faith won't break,
In the sanctity of shared dreams, we wake.

As stars align, our futures beckon,
In whispered prayers, the spirit strengthens.
Bound by purpose, our souls entwine,
In the sanctity of shared dreams, we shine.

With every challenge, with every tear,
In laughter's echo, we draw near.
Through trials faced, our hopes remain,
In the sanctity of shared dreams, no pain.

So let us journey, hand in hand,
In the heart of creation, we take our stand.
In love's reflection, our dreams ignite,
In the sanctity of shared dreams, we find light.

Heavenly Whispers of Once

In the quiet of night, stars surely sing,
Echoes of love that eternity brings.
Gentle spirits roam, guiding our hearts,
In sacred moments, where holy light starts.

Angels in shadows, their wings softly tread,
Carrying prayers where the faithful have fled.
Hand in hand, we rise, past the veil's gentle gleam,
Bound by the whispers of an unbroken dream.

Voices from heaven, in harmony weave,
Every soul cherished, in grace to believe.
A tapestry woven with care and with grace,
Together we journey, to our rightful place.

Each tear that we shed is a drop of pure grace,
Washing away doubts, as we seek His embrace.
In moments of silence, we feel His soft kiss,
A blessing bestowed, a promise of bliss.

From the depths of our hearts, we long to unite,
In the warmth of His love, we bask in the light.
Heavenly whispers, now echo and soar,
Binding our spirits forever, evermore.

The Divine Communion of Souls

In the garden of faith, where spirits entwine,
The breath of existence, a love so divine.
Through ages eternal, our stories unfold,
Tales of compassion, of courage retold.

Gathered together, we rise with the dawn,
Under the heavens, our fears gently drawn.
Hands clasped in prayer, we seek what is true,
In the presence of grace, old paths we renew.

With each heartbeat whispered, a promise we hold,
The flame of our spirits, forever, behold.
Eternal connections that never do wane,
Binding us gently, through laughter and pain.

When shadows encircle, and doubts start to creep,
We turn to each other, our faith we shall keep.
In the divine tapestry, rich and alive,
Together as one, we flourish and thrive.

From the silence of hearts, truth starts to ascend,
In the sacred communion, our spirits transcend.
With love as our beacon, we venture and seek,
In the arms of the heavens, we find strength to speak.

Memories Adrift on Celestial Winds

Like leaves on the breeze, our memories flow,
Carried by starlight, where dreams gently glow.
Each moment a treasure, in hearts gently sown,
Whispers of wisdom, in silence intone.

We wander the cosmos, hand in hand with the past,
Eclipsing the shadows, anchoring fast.
In the tapestry woven, our souls intertwine,
Invisible threads, a connection divine.

In stillness we find, the echoes of grace,
The warmth of His love, a familiar embrace.
Through laughter and sorrow, our spirits shall rise,
Embracing the light, as the darkness complies.

Each tear holds a memory, each smile a sigh,
A dance with the heavens, where time passes by.
With every sweet whisper that night gently brings,
We find our communion in the joy that it sings.

As the planets align, we reach for the light,
United in purpose, our souls take their flight.
Memories adrift, on celestial winds,
Together forever, where existence begins.

Seraphic Bonds of Yesteryears

In the stillness of time, our spirits converge,
Tales of devotion and love ever surge.
With each rising sun, new journeys we take,
Seraphic bonds forged, no distance can break.

Glances we share, like stars in the night,
Illuminating paths, guiding our flight.
From twilight to dawn, in harmony blend,
The legacy written will never, my friend.

In the embrace of the past, where lessons abide,
We find our resilience, our hearts open wide.
Echoes of laughter, resounding through time,
In the chamber of souls, our spirits will climb.

With faith as our compass, we circle around,
In seraphic communion, our hope shall abound.
Though seasons may change, and shadows appear,
The bonds that we form, they always endear.

Through trials and triumphs, we stand hand in hand,
In the grace of the sacred, our hearts understand.
Seraphic bonds of yesteryears shine,
In the depths of our being, forever divine.

The Blessing in Every Memory's Shadow

In quiet moments, whispers speak,
The echoes of love, gentle yet deep.
A sacred bond, unbroken thread,
In every shadow, our hearts are fed.

Through trials faced and laughter shared,
Each memory blooms, a gift declared.
In sorrow's grasp or joy's sweet light,
A blessing glimmers, always in sight.

Let faith's embrace ignite our way,
A guiding hand through night and day.
In every shadow, warmth remains,
Our souls united, free from chains.

With grateful hearts, we weave and spin,
In every loss, a place to begin.
The stories linger, softly told,
In memories bright, our spirits unfold.

So let us walk, hand in hand,
Through life's great journey, a promised land.
In every shadow, love's light guides,
With every blessing, our hope abides.

Threads of Faith Bound in Time

In quiet moments, hands clasped tight,
We weave our dreams, a tapestry bright.
Each thread of faith, a story spun,
In unity found, our hearts are one.

Through trials faced and laughter shared,
The fabric of life, lovingly paired.
With colors rich, through time they blend,
A sacred bond that will not end.

In whispered prayers and songs of grace,
We find our strength, we find our place.
Each woven thread, a line divine,
In every heart, His love does shine.

Together we rise, hand in hand,
Guided by faith, across this land.
The threads of love, so tightly sewn,
In every heart, His truth is known.

For in each stitch, a promise flows,
Of hope eternal, as love bestows.
With every heartbeat, our spirits climb,
Threads of faith bound in endless time.

The Sacred Cadence of Together

In rhythms of life, we find our song,
A sacred cadence that feels so strong.
With every heartbeat, a pulse divine,
In harmony's dance, our souls entwine.

Each moment cherished, each laugh shared,
In sacred circles, our hearts bared.
Through joys and trials, side by side,
In love's embrace, we will abide.

With prayerful whispers, our voices rise,
In gratitude's light, our spirits prize.
Each note of kindness, a gentle grace,
In every heart, His love we trace.

Together we walk, through storm and sun,
In the sacred cadence, we are one.
With every step, His path we seek,
In love's reflection, we find the meek.

So let us journey, hand in hand,
In the sacred rhythm, together we stand.
Each moment a prayer, each heartbeat a chime,
In the sacred cadence of timeless rhyme.

Heartstrings Entwined in Eternal Grace

In the stillness, whispers rise,
Heartstrings entwined, beneath the skies.
In every smile, a spark ignites,
In love's embrace, our hope unites.

Through trials faced, we learn to soar,
In grace bestowed, we find our core.
With hands held tight, we face the storms,
In every shadow, His love transforms.

From dawn to dusk, our spirits blend,
In timeless truth, our hearts transcend.
Each moment shared, a sacred space,
In joy's laughter, we find His grace.

As seasons change, we stand as one,
In every twilight, the day is done.
With grateful hearts, we rise anew,
In eternal grace, our love shines through.

So let us walk, hand in hand,
Through life's vast journey, a promised land.
Heartstrings entwined, in every trace,
Together we bask in His embrace.

The Resurrection of Shared Smiles

In the dawn of love's embrace,
Hope springs forth, a gentle grace.
With laughter soft, we intertwine,
Hearts restored through the divine.

Together, we lift spirits high,
In every tear, a joyful sigh.
From shadows deep, our light ascends,
The warmth of faith that never ends.

As flowers bloom in sunlit skies,
The echoes of our joy arise.
With every smile, a promise made,
In unity, our paths won't fade.

Casting doubts to winds of fate,
Each moment shared, we celebrate.
In our embrace, the world takes flight,
Resurrection in the sacred light.

Bound by love, through trials we tread,
In shared smiles, our spirits fed.
With every glance, our souls ignite,
Together, we bask in holy light.

Remorse in Reverent Stillness

In the hush where echoes fade,
Silent prayers of hearts displayed.
With heavy hearts, we kneel and cry,
Seeking solace in the sky.

The weight of sins, like shadows cast,
In solemn silence, we hold fast.
With tears that fall like sacred rain,
Each drop a token of our pain.

In the stillness, forgiveness sought,
For grace, we plead, our battles fought.
In reverence, we seek to mend,
A broken heart, a faithful friend.

The whispers of redemption call,
In quiet moments, we stand tall.
With outstretched hands toward the light,
We marvel at the gift of sight.

Through humble prayer, we find our way,
In remorse, a brighter day.
United in the strength of trust,
Our spirits lift from sacred dust.

The Last Supper of Shared Time

Gathered 'round the table blessed,
In every glance, our hearts confess.
The warmth of love, in bread and wine,
A memory shared, forever divine.

With laughter sweet, we share our dreams,
In whispered hopes, the future gleams.
Each story told, a bond we weave,
In every moment, we believe.

The weight of time, a gentle sigh,
With every toast, we raise the sky.
In cherished memories, we find grace,
A sacred space, our happy place.

Through trials faced, we re-affirm,
In unity, our spirits burn.
As seasons change, our love remains,
In shared time, our hope sustains.

With gratitude, our voices rise,
In every prayer, the heart complies.
The last supper of days gone by,
In each embrace, love's lullaby.

Ethereal Bonds of Unity

In the stillness of the night,
Whispers of love take gentle flight.
Through unseen strands, we are entwined,
A tapestry of heart and mind.

In every breath, a sacred vow,
Together we stand, here and now.
With courage found in shared embrace,
We seek the light, we find our place.

Beyond the veil, our spirits soar,
Ethereal bonds that we explore.
In moments cherished, we create,
A unity that conquers fate.

Through trials faced and battles won,
In harmony, we rise as one.
With open hearts, we feel the call,
In love, we flourish, never fall.

In sacred spaces, our dreams align,
In every heartbeat, love will shine.
Together, we transcend all strife,
Eternal bonds that bring us life.

An Acolyte's Remembrance

In prayer, the hum of angels soar,
We gather in faith, hearts to explore.
The light within, a candle's gleam,
An acolyte, igniting the dream.

With sacred oil, we bless the way,
Each step, a promise, where spirits sway.
The altar shines with offerings pure,
In unity, our souls endure.

Recalling whispers of silent grace,
In worship's arms, we find our place.
Through trials faced, we rise anew,
An acolyte's path, forever true.

And in the twilight, shadows cast,
Memories linger, holding fast.
With every echo, voices blend,
In reverence, our hearts transcend.

So let us walk, hand in hand,
Through faith and love, a sacred band.
In every heartbeat, a song shall swell,
An acolyte's tale, we shall tell.

Shadows of the Cherubic Past

Winged whispers in the night,
Guardians of divine light.
Beneath the stars, they softly weave,
Stories of hope, we all believe.

In ancient halls where echoes ring,
Cherubs dance and praises sing.
With every shadow, a prayer is cast,
From moments cherished to ages past.

Their laughter sparkles like morning dew,
In every heart, they ignite the true.
Lost in wonder, we seek to find,
The essence of love, eternally bind.

Through sacred paths, we wander low,
In search of strength with every glow.
With every step, we cherish the past,
In shadows of cherubs, love is vast.

So let us lift our voices high,
Reach for the stars that light the sky.
In remembrance sweet, our spirits stay,
Cherubic wings lead the way.

The Sacred Script of You and Me

In words divine, our story breathes,
Woven ties, love's heart believes.
Each line a promise, each verse a prayer,
In sacred script, our souls laid bare.

The ink we share, like blood divine,
With every letter, our hearts entwine.
In verses chanted, truth shall prevail,
A testament of love that cannot fail.

From dawn till dusk, we write our fate,
In pages fluttering, never late.
With ink of devotion, we etch the dawn,
In sacred ties, we both belong.

Through trials faced, our quills like swords,
In battles won, we find the Lord's.
With each stanza, our spirits soar,
In sacred script, we lose no more.

So side by side, through thick and thin,
In love's embrace, we shall begin.
The sacred script of you and me,
A bond unbroken, eternally free.

Hymns of Heartfelt Harmony

In melodies soft, our spirits rise,
With every note, we touch the skies.
A hymn of love, a gentle call,
In heartfelt harmony, we stand tall.

Voices unite in sacred song,
Together we are, where we belong.
With every breath, we share the grace,
In harmony's light, we find our place.

The rhythm of life, in sync we find,
A tapestry woven, forever aligned.
With every heartbeat, a love profound,
In hymns of silence, beauty is found.

So let us sing, as one, we'll soar,
Through storms and trials, forevermore.
With open hearts, our voices free,
In hymns of harmony, we shall be.

Together we rise, we break the night,
In sacred bonds, we find the light.
With every note, we love and trust,
In heartfelt harmony, we are just.

A Pilgrimage to Past Glories

Through valleys deep, we walk in grace,
Each step we take, a sacred space.
With hearts aglow, we seek the light,
In shadows cast, we find our sight.

The echoes of the saints persist,
In whispered prayers, we find our list.
The road is long, yet we feel whole,
With faith as guide, it stirs our soul.

A journey true, we share as one,
In trials faced, we won't be shunned.
With every stone, a tale unfolds,
In unity, our spirit bold.

For glories past, we lift our voice,
In harmony, we make our choice.
To honor those who paved our way,
With love and hope, we greet the day.

A pilgrimage of heart and mind,
In sacred bonds, our souls aligned.
Together, we shall rise and sing,
A timeless truth, this journey brings.

Holy Footprints in the Sand

Upon the shore where waters meet,
The footprints stand, a path so sweet.
In grains of time, we trace His plan,
Each step a mark, a guide for man.

When storms arise and doubts are cast,
With faith like waves, we'll hold steadfast.
In every tide, His love will flow,
Through trials faced, His grace we sow.

The sun may set, the moon may rise,
Yet in our hearts, His light complies.
Each footprint tells of moments shared,
In whispered love, we are declared.

Together we walk, hand in hand,
Through shifting sands, we understand.
A journey bright, with purpose grand,
In sacred trust, we make our stand.

With every step, we feel Him near,
In waves of peace that calm our fear.
Holy footprints guide our way,
In faith and hope, we choose to stay.

Divine Ember of the Heart

A flicker small, yet burning bright,
In darkest nights, it brings us light.
The ember glows, a sacred fire,
With every breath, we reach higher.

In stillness found, we hear His call,
A gentle whisper, love for all.
With fervent hearts, we seek the flame,
In unity, we rise, proclaim.

The warmth it spreads, a healing grace,
In every soul, we find a face.
Together bound, our spirits soar,
In joy and peace, forevermore.

From heart to heart, the ember spreads,
In hands outstretched, our spirit treads.
A radiant glow in every part,
Together we fan the sacred heart.

Through trials faced, we never wane,
The divine ember will sustain.
In love's embrace, we find our way,
With hearts aflame, we greet the day.

The Gospel of Our Connection

In every glance, a truth we share,
The gospel speaks of love and care.
In every heart, a story blends,
Together, we become true friends.

Our hands entwined, we build anew,
In kindness sown, the world we view.
Each voice a song, a sacred blend,
In harmony, our spirits mend.

Through trials faced, we find our strength,
In unity, we go the length.
The gospel sings of hope's embrace,
In every heart, we find our place.

With open arms, we gather near,
In shared belief, we cast out fear.
Together bound, our souls connect,
In faith and love, we resurrect.

For every soul, a light we find,
The gospel true, it leaves us blind.
To hate, to pain, we rise above,
In every pulse, the call of love.

Eternal Gospel of Connection

In the fabric of creation, we intertwine,
Each soul a thread, sacred design.
In whispers of love, the world we mend,
To the heart of the Spirit, we continually tend.

Through trials of life, our spirits unite,
In shadows of doubt, faith shines bright.
In every breath, a prayer takes flight,
Seeking the truth, in the stillness of night.

Together we rise, hand in hand,
In the garden of hope, we firmly stand.
With grace on our lips and peace in our hearts,
Bound by the love that never departs.

Eternal in purpose, steadfast in grace,
Through storms of despair, we find our place.
In moments of silence, the answers unfold,
In the story of oneness, our spirits are told.

For in the embrace of Divine's embrace,
We find our connection, our sacred space.
Together we journey, with love's gentle sway,
In the eternal gospel, we find our way.

The Light of Our Shared Path

Guided by stars in a celestial dome,
We walk this journey, we call it home.
With hearts aglow, in unity we strive,
In every moment, we keep hope alive.

The light that we share, a torch in the dark,
Ignites our souls, it's a holy spark.
With faith as our anchor and love as our guide,
We traverse the valleys, with spirits allied.

Every footstep echoing, a rhythm divine,
In the circle of life, together we shine.
With grace in our movements, and truth in our hearts,
We honor the journey, as each day imparts.

In laughter and sorrow, in joy and in pain,
We find the blessings, like summer rain.
The light of the dawn, in all that we see,
Illuminates paths for you and for me.

Embrace one another, in love's gentle reign,
In the tapestry woven, no thread is in vain.
For the light of our shared path will never fade,
In the harmony of spirits, our hope is laid.

Remembering the Sanctified Moments

In the silence of dawn, we whisper our prayer,
In the richness of life, we breathe the sacred air.
With gratitude flowing like rivers to sea,
We honor the moments that set our hearts free.

Each smile exchanged, a blessing divine,
In the tapestry woven, our souls intertwine.
Through laughter and tears, in joy and in strife,
We celebrate together, the gift of this life.

The stories we share, in shadows and light,
Create a foundation for faith's gentle flight.
With echoes of wisdom, the ages resound,
In the sanctified spaces, our answers are found.

Remember the love that binds us as one,
Underneath the vastness, the moon, and the sun.
The stories and struggles, the triumphs and fears,
Are seeds of connection that flourish through years.

In every heartbeat, a moment is spun,
In the fabric of spirit, we're never undone.
Embrace the sanctified, with eyes open wide,
For in every remembrance, the love will abide.

Spiritually Intertwined

In the depth of our souls, a dance does unfold,
A sacred communion, stories retold.
United in purpose, in light and in grace,
We walk hand in hand in this luminous space.

Through challenges faced, together we stand,
With love as our compass, we journey this land.
With faith as our fortress, we weather the storm,
In the embrace of the Spirit, we find our warm.

Each heartbeat a whisper, each glance a bond,
In the tapestry of life, of which we're so fond.
Spiritually intertwined by the threads of our fate,
In the wisdom of ages, we patiently wait.

Through seasons of change, together we grow,
With kindness and compassion, our hearts overflow.
In the language of love, we each play a part,
In the harmony echoing deep in our heart.

In the journey of life, side by side we tread,
With joy in our steps and faith as our thread.
For together we shine, like stars in the night,
In the embrace of connection, we find pure delight.

Sanctified Moments of Togetherness

In quiet halls where shadows meet,
We gather close, my heart your seat.
With gentle grace, our spirits blend,
In harmony, our voices send.

Each moment shared, a sacred breath,
In love's embrace, we conquer death.
With hands entwined, we forge a bond,
In faith's embrace, our souls respond.

Through trials faced, we rise anew,
Together strong, in all we do.
With humble hearts, our prayers ascend,
In togetherness, our lives transcend.

In laughter's light and sorrow's shade,
Each step we take, our love parades.
With every whisper, we declare,
Our journey blessed, a sacred care.

As time unfolds, we stand as one,
With love's warm glow, there's nothing done.
In sanctified moments, true and bright,
Our souls entwined, in love's pure light.

The Hallelujah of Our Affection

In every glance, I see the grace,
Your love, a light in this vast space.
With gentle words, we share our dreams,
In holy hymns, our passion beams.

Through trials faced, we sing in tune,
In joy and pain, beneath the moon.
Our hearts, a symphony divine,
In hallelujahs, love entwined.

In whispered secrets, love we seek,
In tender moments, souls speak.
With every beat, our rhythm clear,
In faith, we bask, our hearts sincere.

Each sunset paints our spirits bright,
In colors bold, we find our light.
With gratitude, we lift our hands,
In love's embrace, our spirit stands.

Through every storm, we hold the flame,
In faith and love, we rise the same.
The hallelujah of our hearts,
In every breath, our journey starts.

Serene Sanctum of Our Spirits

Within the stillness, we abide,
In tranquil peace, our souls reside.
With eyes of love, we softly gaze,
In serene shadows, our hearts blaze.

In gentle whispers, truth revealed,
In sacred trust, our wounds are healed.
With every touch, the spirit's flow,
In harmony, we learn to grow.

Through sacred paths that we have walked,
In silence shared, our hearts have talked.
A refuge found, in love's embrace,
In every moment, divine grace.

As seasons change and time unfolds,
In nature's arms, our faith upholds.
With every sigh, we breathe the night,
In sacred spaces, hearts take flight.

In quietude, we seek the divine,
In every heartbeat, love's design.
The serene sanctum, our spirits soar,
With every whisper, we adore.

Whispered Prayers of Longing

In the hush of night, a prayer ascends,
For love's embrace that never ends.
With whispered hopes, our spirits rise,
In longing hearts, the truth belies.

With yearning souls, we seek the light,
In shadows cast, we find our right.
With every breath, a quiet plea,
To share our nights, our destiny.

In distant dreams, our hearts entwine,
In sacred thoughts, our love aligns.
With gentle grace, we send our cries,
In heartfelt prayers, where longing lies.

As stars above begin to gleam,
In twilight's glow, we share our dream.
With faith in hand, we journey far,
In whispered prayers, we're never charred.

In every moment, pure and deep,
Our longing finds a sacred keep.
In love's embrace, our spirits soar,
With whispered prayers, forevermore.

The Spirit of Togetherness Illuminated

In the dawn's embrace we stand,
With open hearts, a humble band.
Together we rise, hand in hand,
Guided by love, a sacred land.

Voices united, a timeless song,
In harmony we grow, we belong.
In light we gather, bold and strong,
Together, where we know we throng.

With laughter shared, our spirits soar,
In grace we find the open door.
Embracing all, forevermore,
In togetherness, we shall explore.

In trials faced, we find our might,
Through storms we journey, into light.
Faith unwavering, hearts so bright,
In togetherness, we hold the night.

The bonds we forge, a tapestry,
Woven with threads of unity.
In every soul, a plea set free,
Together, in love's harmony.

Odes of Devotion Under Heaven's Gaze

Beneath the sky, our hearts align,
In silent prayer, your hand in mine.
Together we seek, a path divine,
In love's embrace, our spirits entwine.

With every breath, a chant we make,
In each soft whisper, souls awake.
Our devotion strong, for love's sweet sake,
Under heaven's gaze, we will not break.

Through trials faced, our spirits rise,
In unity strong, we touch the skies.
With faith as wings, we shall surmise,
Ode to the love that never dies.

In morning's light, our promise spun,
In twilight's glow, we are as one.
With every step, our journey's begun,
Under heaven's gaze, the night's just fun.

Forever bound in sacred trust,
Together strengthened, hearts combust.
In this devotion, we are robust,
Under heaven's gaze, we find what's just.

The Pilgrimage of Shared Dreams

On paths unknown, our dreams take flight,
With every step, we seek the light.
In every heartbeat, a wish ignites,
Together we journey, through day and night.

Hand in hand, we traverse the lands,
Each shared vision, like golden strands.
In silence whispers, love understands,
United in hope, our fate commands.

Through valleys low, and mountains high,
In laughter shared, we touch the sky.
Each dream a spark, we cannot deny,
On this pilgrimage, we learn to fly.

In every challenge, we find our grace,
In every struggle, a warm embrace.
Together we rise, we find our place,
In shared dreams, we feel God's trace.

With every dawn, new dreams align,
In unity, our spirits shine.
As pilgrims, our hearts intertwine,
In this journey, our souls combine.

Celestial Bonds Awakening in Reverence

In the hush of night, our spirits call,
Beneath the stars, we stand in thrall.
Awakening bonds that never fall,
In reverence deep, we give our all.

With every heartbeat, love's pulse shown,
In gentle whispers, we are not alone.
Celestial ties that ever have grown,
In sacred silence, our hearts are known.

Each moment shared, a treasured grace,
In the dance of time, we find our place.
Awakening prayers that hearts embrace,
In reverence, we weave love's space.

Through trials faced, we strengthen the chain,
In unity's song, we rise again.
Celestial bonds, a sacred refrain,
In these moments, we break the pain.

Together we walk, hand in hand,
With every step, a solemn stand.
In reverence true, forever planned,
Celestial bonds, our life's demand.

The Choir of Our Collective Heartbeat

In harmony we rise and sing,
A chorus of devotion's cling.
Each voice a note in divine grace,
Together we find our sacred space.

Through trials faced, our spirits soar,
In unity, we seek much more.
With every pulse, a sacred art,
The melody of each pure heart.

Resounding in the quiet night,
Our prayers ascend, a beacon's light.
A symphony of love and tears,
Echoing through the coming years.

In every breath, we feel the bond,
A testament to what we've donned.
With faith as our eternal guide,
Together, we walk side by side.

Blessed by the rhythm of our souls,
A sacred dance where each one rolls.
In the choir of our devout call,
We find our strength; we shall not fall.

Celestial Promises in the Mirror of Time

Reflections gleam on sacred shores,
Promises made, our spirits soar.
In each embrace, we write our fate,
A timeline wrought with love so great.

Stars gaze down with watchful eyes,
Whispering secrets from the skies.
Each passing moment, a gift we share,
In the mirror of time, we find our prayer.

Through valleys deep and mountains high,
We trace our steps, and yet we fly.
Bound by hope, through joy and strife,
Each moment echoes, the song of life.

Our vows inscribed on the pages turned,
In the flame of faith, our hearts have burned.
Celestial dreams dance in the night,
Guided by love's eternal light.

As we journey through shadows cast,
With every heartbeat, love will last.
In time's embrace, together we stand,
Celestial promises, forever hand in hand.

Lanterns of Love Guiding Our Path

In the darkness, lanterns glow,
Radiant warmth, love's gentle flow.
They light our way through untold night,
Guiding us with faith's pure light.

Each step we take, hand in hand,
Together we rise, together we stand.
Through storms and trials, we shall remain,
Carried by love, through joy and pain.

With every flicker, a promise made,
In the journey, not afraid.
Our hearts aflame, a guiding spark,
Lanterns blazing in the dark.

In the tapestry of our shared days,
We weave our hopes in myriad ways.
With love as our compass, we'll never part,
Always driven by a faithful heart.

As the dawn breaks upon our lives,
The lanterns shine, our spirit thrives.
With love's guidance, we find our way,
Lanterns of hope in bright array.

Chronicles of a Faithful Union

In the chapters of a life we weave,
Stories of hope that we believe.
Each page reflects the love we grow,
In the currents of time's soft flow.

Bonded by dreams, our hearts align,
In the silence, your hand in mine.
Together we write the verses true,
Chronicles etched in skies of blue.

Through trials faced, our spirits blend,
In love's embrace, we learn to mend.
Each challenge met, a lesson learned,
In the fires of faith, our hearts have burned.

With every breath, we build our story,
In whispered prayers, we find our glory.
United as one, through thick and thin,
Chronicles of love, our sacred hymn.

Time may turn with gentle grace,
Yet in your eyes, my sacred place.
In the faithful union, we forever stay,
Writing chronicles, come what may.

Eternal Echoes of Togetherness

In the stillness of the night, we pray,
Hearts entwined, seeking the light each day.
Whispers of love in the sacred air,
Together we tread, in faith we share.

Voices rise like a gentle breeze,
Carried forth on the ancient trees.
Mirrored souls in the vast expanse,
In unity's dance, we find our stance.

Threads of hope in a tapestry spun,
Each moment cherished, we are as one.
Through trials faced, we hold on tight,
Eternal echoes guide our flight.

Stars above, like blessings, shine bright,
Leading us home with their soft, warm light.
In a circle of grace, we gather near,
In harmony's song, there's nothing to fear.

Love's embrace in the dawn's first glow,
Together we rise, united we flow.
In prayerful whispers, our spirits soar,
Eternal echoes, forevermore.

Sacred Whispers of a Shared Journey

Underneath the vast, embracing sky,
We walk together, you and I.
Each step a promise, each breath a song,
In sacred whispers, we both belong.

Through valleys low and mountains steep,
Our journey woven, for love so deep.
In shared silence, our hearts align,
In every heartbeat, a glimpse divine.

As dawn paints colors on morning's face,
We find our rhythm, a holy grace.
With every challenge, together we rise,
In sacred whispers, we touch the skies.

Miracles bloom where faith finds root,
In the bond of our journey, we find our truth.
Hand in hand, through storms we'll steer,
In sacred whispers, the path is clear.

Together we gather the dreams we hold,
In stories spoken, our love unfolds.
As stars bear witness to time's soft call,
In sacred whispers, we cherish it all.

Threads of Light Woven in Unity

With every dawn, the light grows bright,
In threads of hope, we unite our plight.
Stitching moments with love's gentle grace,
In unity's fabric, we find our place.

A tapestry woven with hearts so bold,
In the warmth of friendship, our spirits unfold.
Each knot a prayer, each line a vow,
Together we stand, here and now.

In storms we gather, a fortress of care,
Threads of compassion in the cool night air.
Woven together through trials we face,
In threads of light, we discover grace.

The past and future meld into one,
In the fabric of time, our lives are spun.
With joy and wisdom, together we weave,
In threads of light, a gift to believe.

So let's stitch our dreams with courage and might,
In every heart shines a beacon of light.
Together we craft a masterpiece grand,
In threads of light, forever we stand.

Divine Remembrance in the Quiet Hours

In the quiet hours, when twilight falls,
We gather in silence, heeding the calls.
Thoughts of the sacred gently arise,
In divine remembrance, our spirits sigh.

With candles lit, we share our grace,
In heartfelt whispers, we find our space.
Every prayer a step on our path sincere,
In the stillness of love, we draw ever near.

The echoes of laughter, the warmth of tears,
In divine remembrance, we conquer fears.
Holding the moments, both bitter and sweet,
In our hearts' chambers, the past we greet.

Merging together in the folds of time,
In the rhythm of life, our souls will rhyme.
Each heartbeat a note in the sacred choir,
In divine remembrance, we lift higher.

As night entwines the heavens above,
We rest in the comfort of endless love.
In the quiet hours, our hearts take flight,
In divine remembrance, we unite.

Chronicles of Unity Written in the Stars

In the heavens high, our fates align,
Whispers of old beckon through the night.
Stars waltz together, their paths divine,
Guiding our hearts, igniting the light.

From distant realms where dreams take flight,
The tapestry glows with stories untold.
Each twinkle a promise, a spark of insight,
Knit by the hands of the wise and bold.

Unseen forces bind us in grace,
A chorus of souls in harmony sing.
Through trials we traverse, we find our place,
In unity's glow, our spirits take wing.

The time-worn words echo through the ages,
Faith written boldly on the scroll of night.
With every heartbeat, destiny engages,
Bright constellations, our guiding light.

So let us gather, in reverence stand,
Beneath the vast canvas, wisdom unfolds.
As chronicles weave through the heavens so grand,
In unity's embrace, our future beholds.

In the Sanctuary of Time's Embrace

In the stillness of dawn, where shadows play,
Time unfolds gently, a sacred space.
Moments linger, then drift away,
Cradled by silence, we find our place.

The echoes of ages whisper and call,
Each heartbeat reverberates, lessons to learn.
In the sanctuary's warmth, we rise and fall,
Fires of faith within us burn.

Beneath the arching sky, stories bloom,
As seasons change, so do hearts entwined.
In the light of grace, dispelling gloom,
We gather together, our destinies aligned.

Branches woven with hopes long foretold,
Rooted in love, the past we embrace.
In time's vast continuum, we are bold,
Chasing the light, an eternal chase.

So let us cherish the moments we find,
In the sanctuary where souls unite.
With every breath, a treasure confined,
In time's rich embrace, we shine ever bright.

The Sacred Garden of Our Past

In the garden where memories bloom anew,
Petals of yesteryears whisper and sigh.
Each fragile blossom, a story in view,
Rooted in soil where our dreams lie.

Through paths of remembrance, we gently tread,
Amidst the shadows, grace fills the air.
Nurtured by love, what once lay dead,
Transforms into beauty, our burdens to bear.

The fragrance of kindness wafts from each tree,
Branches adorned with the fruits of our toil.
In the sacred garden, we wander free,
Harvesting wisdom from life's fertile soil.

Seasons may fade, yet our hearts stay bold,
Holding the stories that time can't erase.
In the garden, the warmth of love unfolds,
Blessings reflected in every embrace.

So plant the seeds of hope deep within,
Water them softly with faith's gentle rain.
In the sacred garden, let life begin,
As past and present dance together again.

Divine Echoes in the Hall of Memory

In the hall of echoes, memories resound,
Whispers of laughter and shadows of tears.
Each step we take leaves a mark on the ground,
Carved by the hands of our hopes and fears.

Through corridors painted with colors of grace,
Footfalls like prayers echo through the air.
In every corner, we find our place,
As love's gentle hand mends the wear and tear.

The tapestry woven, rich in our song,
Threads of connection, both fragile and strong.
In the hall of memory, we all belong,
Together we gather, where spirits prolong.

With each passing moment, we capture the light,
Illuminating tales of our journey in time.
In the sacred space, darkness takes flight,
Each heartbeat a rhythm, each whisper a rhyme.

So let us remember, as long as we live,
The divine echoes that weave through our soul.
In the hall of memory, we have much to give,
Together in love, we eternally whole.

The Soul's Testament of Love

In whispers soft, our hearts unite,
Bound by a love that shines so bright.
With every prayer, our spirits rise,
A testament that never lies.

Through trials faced, hand in hand,
Together we stand, on sacred land.
In every tear, there's grace we find,
A love eternal, pure and blind.

In moments vast, and still, so small,
We seek His wisdom, hear His call.
With each heartbeat, we become whole,
The essence of love, the soul's true goal.

A garden blooms within our souls,
Where kindness waters, and faith controls.
In every shadow, light breaks through,
A testament of love, ever new.

When night descends, and doubts arise,
We find our strength beneath the skies.
In prayer, our voices intertwine,
A sacred bond, forever divine.

Pillars of Faith

In every storm, we find our ground,
With pillars firm, our hope is found.
Through trials fierce, we stand upright,
Embraced in love, surrounded by light.

From ancient texts, wisdom flows,
A guiding star, as faith bestows.
Through sacred words, our spirits soar,
Together we seek, forevermore.

With every prayer, our hearts ignite,
A flame that warms, a holy light.
In trusting hands, we place our cares,
Rising above, like whispered prayers.

In community, our strength is found,
A tapestry rich, with love unbound.
Each soul a thread, uniquely spun,
As pillars stand, our journey's won.

With every challenge, we grow strong,
United together, we all belong.
In shadows deep, a guiding grace,
Our pillars of faith, in time and space.

Memories Aligned

In quiet moments, memories bloom,
Like fragrant flowers in a room.
Through paths we've walked, side by side,
With faith as our compass, love our guide.

In laughter shared, our spirits dance,
Each memory crafted, a timeless chance.
With joy and pain, we weave the thread,
In every story, our hearts are fed.

With gentle hands, we hold the past,
Cherishing moments, forever to last.
Within our hearts, echoes of grace,
Memories aligned, in sacred space.

As seasons change, we stand as one,
In every dusk, a rising sun.
With gratitude deep, we treasure each day,
In the light of love, we find our way.

Through whispered prayers, our journeys blend,
With every heartbeat, our lives transcend.
In the tapestry woven, memories shine,
Aligned in faith, eternally divine.

In the Light of Togetherness

In twilight's glow, we find our peace,
A bond so strong, may it never cease.
With hearts entwined, in love we bask,
Together we rise, united we ask.

In grace we gather, hand in hand,
A chorus of hope across the land.
With every smile, our spirits grow,
In the light of togetherness, we glow.

In trials faced, we share a tear,
A sacred bond, forever near.
Within our souls, a spark ignites,
Together we shine, through darkest nights.

With open hearts, we let love flow,
In every moment, our faith will show.
In the light of joy, we find our way,
Together we stand, come what may.

With kindness shared, we build the bridge,
Through faith unbroken, we shall not smidge.
In togetherness, our dreams align,
A journey of hearts, forever divine.

Threads of Grace in Our Tapestry

In every thread, a story spun,
A tapestry woven, for everyone.
With colors bright, and textures bold,
Threads of grace, in warmth enfold.

Through laughter shared, and sorrows deep,
Our hearts are stitched, in memories we keep.
In woven paths, our journeys blend,
A sacred bond, that shall not end.

With patience sewn, and kindness sown,
In every stitch, love has grown.
In threads of grace, we find our way,
A masterpiece crafted, day by day.

Through trials faced, with faith we stand,
With open hearts, we hold His hand.
In unity strong, our dreams take flight,
A tapestry rich, in purest light.

So let us weave, in harmony's song,
In threads of grace, we all belong.
With every heartbeat, our love will shine,
A tapestry sacred, forever divine.

Sacrament of Shared Laughter

In joy we gather, hearts allied,
With laughter's echo, spirits glide.
A sacred bond, in joy we beam,
United here, a holy dream.

With each shared jest, the veil is thin,
A glimpse of grace, where love begins.
We raise our voices, pure delight,
In laughter's rhythm, day turns bright.

The holy spark in smiles we share,
A testament, our love laid bare.
In sacred moments, blessings flow,
In shared laughter, our spirits grow.

For joy is prayer, a sacred gift,
In laughter's sway, our souls uplift.
We dance in light, with hearts so free,
A sacrament of unity.

Together we tread this holy ground,
In every chuckle, peace is found.
Let laughter reign, our voices soar,
In unity, we seek much more.

The Covenant of Our Days

In morning light, our hearts align,
A sacred bond, the love divine.
With every breath, we weave our fate,
In trust we stand, we elevate.

Through trials faced, we hold on tight,
With faith as guide, we claim the night.
Each whispered prayer, a promise made,
In every step, our doubts allayed.

As seasons turn and shadows shift,
We find in love, our greatest gift.
In laughter's warmth, in sorrow's tear,
Our covenant grows, forever dear.

Through days of sun, through storms of grace,
We walk together, face to face.
In every hour, our spirits rise,
A testament beneath the skies.

With open hearts, we share our dreams,
In unity, our passion teems.
In sacred vows, our lives unfold,
In every moment, love retold.

Cherished Incense of Intentions

In quietude, our hearts intone,
With whispered hopes, our love is sown.
Each prayer ascends, like fragrant smoke,
In sacred silence, spirits provoke.

With every thought, a seed we plant,
In faith we nurture, our spirits chant.
Through trials faced, our strength prevails,
In heartfelt whispers, love never fails.

The incense rises, soft and sweet,
A bridge of love, our souls repeat.
In every breath, a promise stirs,
An echo of hope, in hearts and prayers.

As shadows fall, we stand in light,
Our intentions pure, our goals in sight.
With every moment, we hold dear,
The sacred bond that draws us near.

From deepest prayers, our purpose blooms,
In cherished dreams, dispelling glooms.
With incense rising, hearts ignite,
In sacred space, we find our might.

Faith's Subtle Embrace

In gentle whispers, soft and near,
Faith cradles hearts, dispelling fear.
A tender touch, a guiding hand,
In sacred trust, together we stand.

Through burdens shared, our souls repair,
In faith's embrace, we find our care.
With every step, we walk the line,
In grace we find, our spirits shine.

With open hearts, our stories blend,
In every struggle, love transcends.
Through trials faced, we rise above,
In unity, we share our love.

In moments quiet, blessings flow,
In subtle faith, we learn and grow.
Through gentle sighs, our spirits soar,
In faith's embrace, we seek for more.

Through every dawn, through every night,
Faith holds us close, a guiding light.
In every heartbeat, sacred grace,
Together we find, faith's warm embrace.

Angels of Our Better Days

In light they descend, our guardians fair,
With wings spread wide, banishing despair.
They guide our souls through trials and fears,
Their whispers envelop, wiping our tears.

Each dawn they bring a promise so bright,
With hope revived, in the morning light.
They lift our hearts to dreams once delayed,
Angels soar high, in our hearts they wade.

In laughter's embrace, their joy we find,
In every smile, love intertwined.
Through valleys deep and mountains so high,
Angels of grace will never say goodbye.

Reverie of Kindred Spirits

In the stillness, souls entwine,
Hearts resonate, a bond divine.
Together we drift on dreams soft-spun,
In the realm of love, we are forever one.

Every glance, a promise we share,
In the silent night, tender and rare.
Through the shadows, our light will blaze,
Kindred spirits in a sacred maze.

With laughter and tears, our journey flows,
In fields of grace, our connection grows.
Companions of fate, through thick and thin,
In this reverie, true light begins.

Reflections in Holy Waters

In tranquil streams where stillness reigns,
We find our truths, release our chains.
With every ripple, prayers shall rise,
Reflecting grace beneath the skies.

The depths reveal our souls so bare,
In holy waters, we find our prayer.
Each wave a blessing, each splash a song,
In nature's arms, where we belong.

As sunlit glimmers dance on the face,
We seek redemption, we seek His grace.
Through waters pure, our spirits ascend,
In faith's embrace, our hearts shall mend.

The Whispering Tabernacle of Love

In hushed corners, where hearts collide,
The whispers of love, we cannot hide.
Each prayer and promise softly shared,
In sacred bonds, we are declared.

The tabernacle of our deepest dreams,
In love's embrace, nothing is as it seems.
With fervent hope, we journey within,
To find the light, the voices of kin.

In the silence, our spirits entwine,
A canvas of grace, a love divine.
Together we stand, unbroken, we thrive,
In this sacred space, our souls come alive.

Celestial Embrace of Two Souls

In the quiet dawn, love's light will shine,
Two hearts entwined, a bond divine.
With whispers soft, they seek the grace,
Bound together in a sacred space.

Through trials faced, they stand so tall,
With faith as guide, they shall not fall.
Each moment shared, a prayer they weave,
In celestial dance, they truly believe.

Their spirits soar, like eagles high,
Unified under the endless sky.
In joy and sorrow, in peace and strife,
Together they journey, this gift of life.

Sanctified Memories in the Heart's Temple

Within the heart, where memories dwell,
Sanctified whispers, a love's sweet spell.
In every tear, a lesson learned,
In every joy, the flame has burned.

Two souls entwined like sacred vines,
In each heartbeat, their story shines.
Echoes of laughter fill the air,
A hallowed space, a love laid bare.

With every glance, the past unfolds,
A tapestry woven, rich with golds.
In twilight's glow, they find the way,
To cherish moments, come what may.

A Covenant of Stars in the Night Sky

Under the stars, they pledge their hearts,
In the cool night, where silence imparts.
Each twinkle a promise, a love so bright,
Guiding their path through the darkest night.

With hands held high, they seek the light,
In the galaxy's grace, their spirits take flight.
Bound by the cosmos, their souls entwined,
In this celestial realm, true love defined.

As constellations tell their tale,
Two wanderers brave, they shall not fail.
For every star wishes them well,
In the universe, their love shall swell.

The Altar of Our Emotions

At the altar of love, their hearts reside,
With every breath, they choose to abide.
In faith's embrace, they find their peace,
With every promise, their joy will increase.

Each tear a testament, each laugh a song,
In the sacred space, where they belong.
Their spirits woven like threads of gold,
A bond unbroken, a love to hold.

In stillness met, where silence speaks,
They share their truth as the heart seeks.
With hands of trust, they build their way,
In the altar of emotions, come what may.

Milton Keynes UK
Ingram Content Group UK Ltd.
UKHW022223251124
451566UK00006B/101

9 789916 792094